SPINNING CIRCLES:
Action Poems

Written and illustrated by Raven Howell

Photography by Vid Mednis

Bookstand Publishing

www.bookstandpublishing.com

Published by
Bookstand Publishing
Morgan Hill, CA 95037
4383_3

ISBN 978-1-63498-285-6

Library of Congress Control Number: 2015920799

Printed in the United States of America

SPINNING CIRCLES:
Action Poems

Written and illustrated by Raven Howell

Photography by Vid Mednis

For Maris and Jakob, who always keep me in motion

A special dedication to Dick, my inspiration for "Grampa's Day"

The poem, "Snow Storm" was first published in the Jan/Feb 2011 issue of Pockets

Also by Raven Howell

Dozy Poems, Cozy Days
Illustrated by Maris Howell

CONTENTS

SPINNING CIRCLES:
Action Poems

SPINNING CIRCLES

I spin around in circles,
My arms toward open sky;
The wind lifts them like feathered wings –
I feel like I could fly!

I spin around in circles.
I glide, I sail, I soar.
I spin around in circles
'Til I can turn no more.
Topsy-turvy, weeble-wobble
Drop down to the ground,
And now though *I* no longer move
The sky still spins around!

BALL

I kick it.
I roll it.
It bounces off the wall.
I toss it in the air,
I reach and catch my ball,
And sometimes
- my puppy does!

A SEE SAW RHYME

Slowly rising,
Up I go,
Then touching down
On tippy-toe.

Dipping low,
Springing high,
See-sawing
From earth to sky!

MAKING MUSIC

Clap your hands,
Twirl and dance;
Giddy-up, giddy-up,
Leap and prance!

Tap a drum,
Pluck a string,
Toot a flute
And sing, sing, sing!

WHAT SHOULD WE DO TODAY?

Should we trot like horses?
Clomp, clomp, clomp

Should we trudge like elephants?
Stomp, stomp, stomp

Should we chirp like birds do?
Tweet, tweet, tweet

Should we skip and jump
On our own two feet?

GRAMPA'S DAY

Pick me up to piggyback.
Lift me high
Upon your back.
Ride me, sway me
In the breeze.
Gallop me among the trees.
Grampa, hum my favorite song
While I bounce and bob along.

JUMPING JACK

Thumping,
Bumping
Jumping jack,
Jump to Mexico and back!

North, south,
East, west –
Bouncing,
Flouncing is the best!

Leap-frog, leap-frog
Red, blue, green,
Will you be my jumping bean?

BOX OF BLOCKS

I stack them sideways
Long and wide;
Construct
A roller coaster ride.

I pile them higher
One by one,
And build a tower
To the sun.

I heap them up, and
Out of sight –
My ladder
To the moon at night!

RAINY DAY

Skipping to the rhythm of the rain is fun
While we wait for Mr. Sun.
Sashay 'round in misty gray
Washing clean this gloomy day.

Bang, bang, bang
To the drumming drops.
Rap, rap, rap
'Til the raining stops.

Grass grows greener
As we skip
To the rhythm of the raindrops
As they drip.

FINGER PAINTING

Smear your fingers,
Blot 5 cards.
Streak the sky
With shooting stars.
Paint zigzags,
Splash a square,
Then swirl lines
To make a bear.
Use your thumb,
Smudge a sun –
And to think....
You've just begun!

SAND

I curl my fingers,
Cup my hand.
Spoon in - scoop out
Silky sand.

I fill my pail
Up to the top.
Dig, dip,
Lift, drop.

Shoo, ladybug!
Shoo, little ants!
Shoo, tickly sand –
Out of my pants!

11

QUICK!

Slip-slide
Over wet grass.
Jump
The sidewalk crack.
Splash
Barefoot in puddles
Before the rain comes back!

FOLLOW THE LEADER

I'm the leader,
Follow me:
Bend your elbow.
Tap your knee.

Stand up tall.
Hike in place.
Put a smile
Upon your face.

Now what would you like to do?
You can be the leader, too!

SOMERSAULTING

Fluff a pillow
On the ground.
Make yourself
A little round.

Tilt your head
As you begin.
Tip and tumble.
Tuck your chin.

Over now –
Heels in the air.
Somersault
If you dare!

BATH TIME

Chug-a-chug
Chug-a-chug
Little tugboat

Chug-a-chug
Chug-a-chug
Glide and float

Chug-a-chug
Chug-a-chug
It's just me

Chug-a-chug
Chug-a-chug
Sailing the sea.

GAME TIME!

When it rains,
Indoor games –
Puzzles, ping pong,
Cards, charades.

Today the weather's
Nice outside,
We run and tag,
And seek and hide.

Kick the ball,
Run to base,
Whack that bat,
Keep the pace!

We swing and jump,
And laugh some more,
Even our dog plays
Tug-of-war!

DUCK, DUCK, GOOSE

We sit in a circle, playing the game,
Get up and race
If we're tapped the "goose" name.

Hurry, and try to tag back if you can!
Then return to the "duck" space
Where you began.

Ducks just remain, but geese always run.
I wait in suspense
'Til *I'm* picked as the one!

CATCH YOUR BREATH

Little inchworm,
Arch and turn.
Pinch your green-ness
On the fern.

Inch up on my outstretched finger
Then we both can sit and linger.

FAMILY TREASURES

Babies laugh, babies cry,
They smile hello and wave bye-bye.

They sip, they gurgle, drool and dribble,
Crawl and creep, and screech and scribble.

My sister stands, then plops back down,
She bursts in giggle, burps and frowns.

At last she sleeps, head on my shoulder,
And makes me smile as I hold her.

SNOW STORM

Snowflakes glaze me
Head to toe.
I shimmy, I sparkle,
I romp through the snow.
My mouth opens wide
Catching cold flakes
In the glittering flurry
The falling snow makes.

Then *crackle* and *crunch*,
I stomp ice on the ground.
I make a snow angel
And pack a snow mound.

Ready for cocoa –
It's time to get warm.
We'll come out again
The next snowstorm!

HIDE AND SEEK

I skitter, I flitter,
I leap and pounce.
I reach, I stretch,
And spring, and bounce.
In hide and seek –
It's here and gone,
This firefly
Upon my lawn.

OFF TO BED

Whisper,
Sigh,
Blink your eyes.
Dream in silver lullabies.

Dipped in starlight,
Sleepy head,
Quiet now –
It's off to bed...

CPSIA information can be obtained at www.ICGtesting.com
Printed in the USA
BVIW12n1905021117
499251BV00003BA/12